IAM SURE,

THANKFUL AND

BLESSED.

THIS BOOK
BELONGS TO

ALL THINGS ABOUT ME

MY NAME IS

....

MY FAVORIT

I am ⬭ old

ANIMAL ....

BOOK ....

FOOD ....

HERO ....

MY BRITHDAY

....

I WAS BORN IN

....

PHONE NUMBER

....

I LIVE IN

....

My friend are

....

....

....

....

WHEN I GROW UP
I WILL BE

....

....

I love ♥

....

I hit ✖

....

DATE: MO TU WE TH FR SR ...../..../......

TO DAY I AM THANKFUL FOR

1

3

....
....

....
....

2

....
....

I FEEL

THI PERSEN MAKE ME HAPPY TO DAY

DRAW SOMETHING AWESOME THAT HAPPEND TO DAY

DATE: MO TU WE TH FR SR ...../..../.......

TO DAY I AM THANKFUL FOR

1

3

....
....

....
....

2

....
....

I FEEL

THI PERSEN MAKE ME HAPPY TO DAY

....

DRAW SOMETHING AWESOME THAT HAPPEND TO DAY

DATE: MO TU WE TH FR SR ....../...../......

TO DAY I AM THANKFUL FOR

1

....

....

3

THANK YOU

....

....

2

....

....

I FEEL

THI PERSEN MAKE ME HAPPY TO DAY

....

DRAW SOMETHING AWESOME THAT HAPPEND TO DAY

DATE: MO TU WE TH FR SR ...../..../......

TO DAY I AM THANKFUL FOR

1

3

....
....

....
....

2

....
....

I FEEL

THI PERSEN MAKE ME HAPPY TO DAY

....

DRAW SOMETHING AWESOME THAT HAPPEND TO DAY

DATE: MO TU WE TH FR SR ...../..../......

TO DAY I AM THANKFUL FOR

1

3

2

I FEEL

THI PERSEN MAKE ME HAPPY TO DAY

....

DRAW SOMETHING AWESOME THAT HAPPEND TO DAY

DATE: MO TU WE TH FR SR ...../..../......

TO DAY I AM THANKFUL FOR

1

....
....

3

....
....

2

....
....

THI PERSEN MAKE ME HAPPY TO DAY

....

DRAW SOMETHING AWESOME THAT HAPPEND TO DAY

DATE: MO TU WE TH FR SR ..../..../......

TO DAY I AM THANKFUL FOR

1

....
....

3

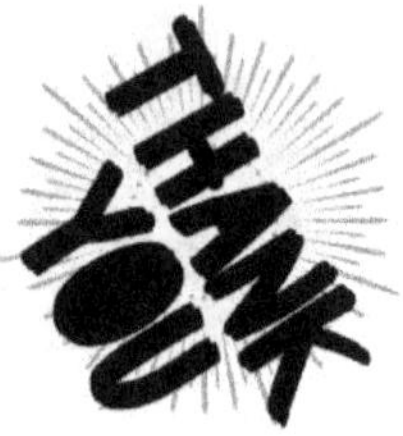

....
....

2

....
....

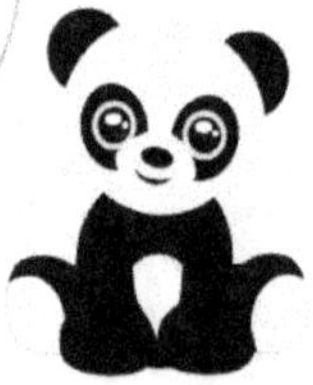

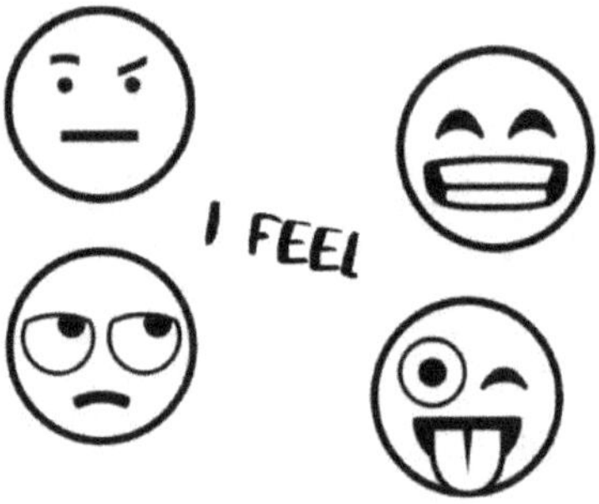

I FEEL

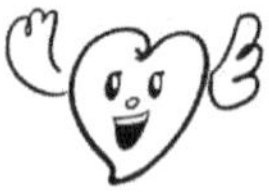

THI PERSEN MAKE ME HAPPY TO DAY ♥

....

DRAW SOMETHING AWESOME THAT HAPPEND TO DAY

....

DATE: MO TU WE TH FR SR ...../..../......

TO DAY I AM THANKFUL FOR

1

3

2

THI PERSEN MAKE ME HAPPY TO DAY

....

DRAW SOMETHING AWESOME THAT HAPPEND TO DAY

DATE: MO TU WE TH FR SR ..../..../......

TO DAY I AM THANKFUL FOR

1

....

....

3

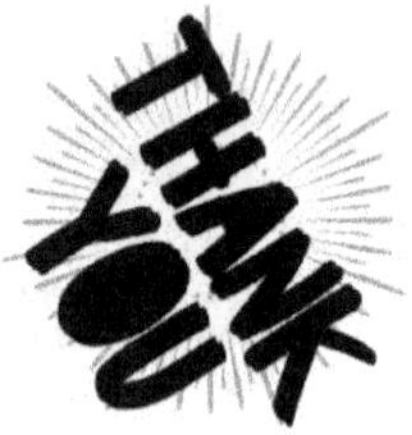

....

....

2

....

....

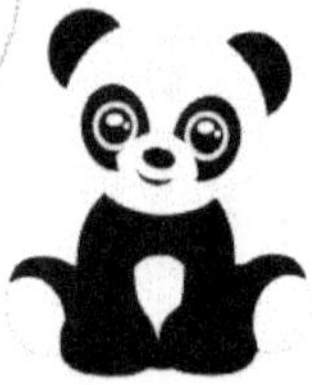

I FEEL

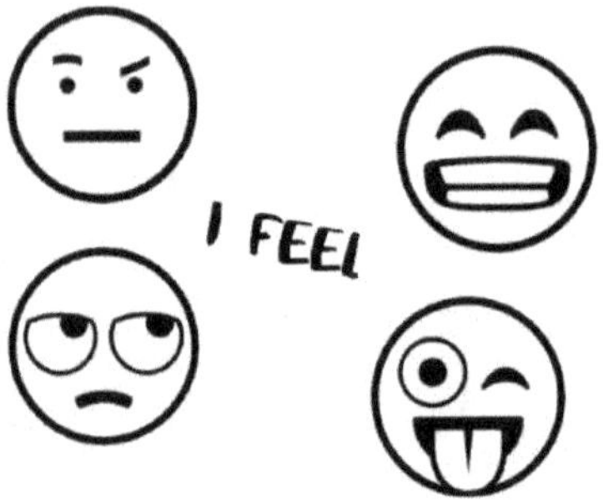

THI PERSEN MAKE ME HAPPY TO DAY

....

DRAW SOMETHING AWESOME THAT HAPPEND TO DAY

DATE: MO TU WE TH FR SR ...../..../......

TO DAY I AM THANKFUL FOR

1

....
....

3

....
....

2

....
....

THI PERSEN MAKE ME HAPPY TO DAY

....

DRAW SOMETHING AWESOME THAT HAPPEND TO DAY

DATE: MO TU WE TH FR SR ...../..../......

TO DAY I AM THANKFUL FOR

1

....
....

3

....
....

2

....
....

I FEEL

THI PERSEN MAKE ME HAPPY TO DAY

....

DRAW SOMETHING AWESOME THAT HAPPEND TO DAY

DATE: MO TU WE TH FR SR ...../..../......

TO DAY I AM THANKFUL FOR

1

....
....

3

....
....

2

....
....

I FEEL

THI PERSEN MAKE ME HAPPY TO DAY

....

DRAW SOMETHING AWESOME THAT HAPPEND TO DAY

DATE: MO TU WE TH FR SR ...../..../......

TO DAY I AM THANKFUL FOR

1

....

....

3

....

....

2

....

....

I FEEL

THI PERSEN MAKE ME HAPPY TO DAY

....

DRAW SOMETHING AWESOME THAT HAPPEND TO DAY

DATE: MO TU WE TH FR SR ...../..../......

TO DAY I AM THANKFUL FOR

1

3

2

I FEEL

THI PERSEN MAKE ME HAPPY TO DAY

....

DRAW SOMETHING AWESOME THAT HAPPEND TO DAY

DATE: MO TU WE TH FR SR ...../..../......

TO DAY I AM THANKFUL FOR

1

....
....

3

....
....

2

....
....

THI PERSEN MAKE ME HAPPY TO DAY

....

DRAW SOMETHING AWESOME THAT HAPPEND TO DAY

DATE: MO TU WE TH FR SR ...../...../.......

TO DAY I AM THANKFUL FOR

● ●

1

3

....

....

....

....

2

....

....

I FEEL

THI PERSEN MAKE ME HAPPY TO DAY

....

DRAW SOMETHING AWESOME THAT HAPPEND TO DAY

DATE: MO TU WE TH FR SR ...../..../......

TO DAY I AM THANKFUL FOR

1

....

....

3

....

....

2

....

....

I FEEL

THI PERSEN MAKE ME HAPPY TO DAY

....

DRAW SOMETHING AWESOME THAT HAPPEND TO DAY

DATE: MO TU WE TH FR SR ...../..../......

TO DAY I AM THANKFUL FOR

1

....

....

3

....

....

2

....

....

I FEEL

THI PERSEN MAKE ME HAPPY TO DAY

....

DRAW SOMETHING AWESOME THAT HAPPEND TO DAY

DATE: MO TU WE TH FR SR ...../...../......

TO DAY I AM THANKFUL FOR

1

....
....

3

....
....

2

....
....

I FEEL

THI PERSEN MAKE ME HAPPY TO DAY

....

DRAW SOMETHING AWESOME THAT HAPPEND TO DAY

DATE: MO TU WE TH FR SR ...../..../......

TO DAY I AM THANKFUL FOR

1

3

2

I FEEL

THI PERSEN MAKE ME HAPPY TO DAY

DRAW SOMETHING AWESOME THAT HAPPEND TO DAY

DATE: MO TU WE TH FR SR ...../..../......

TO DAY I AM THANKFUL FOR

THI PERSEN MAKE ME HAPPY TO DAY

DRAW SOMETHING AWESOME THAT HAPPEND TO DAY

DATE: MO TU WE TH FR SR ..../..../......

TO DAY I AM THANKFUL FOR

1

3

2

I FEEL

THI PERSEN MAKE ME HAPPY TO DAY

DRAW SOMETHING AWESOME THAT HAPPEND TO DAY

DATE: MO TU WE TH FR SR ...../..../......

TO DAY I AM THANKFUL FOR

1

....

....

3

....

....

2

....

....

I FEEL

THI PERSEN MAKE ME HAPPY TO DAY

....

DRAW SOMETHING AWESOME THAT HAPPEND TO DAY

DATE: MO TU WE TH FR SR ...../...../......

TO DAY I AM THANKFUL FOR

● ● ● ● ● ● ● ● ● ● ● ● ● ● ● ● ● ● ● ●

1

3

....
....

....
....

2

....
....

THI PERSEN MAKE ME HAPPY TO DAY

....

DRAW SOMETHING AWESOME THAT HAPPEND TO DAY

DATE: MO TU WE TH FR SR ...../..../......

TO DAY I AM THANKFUL FOR

1

3

2

I FEEL

THI PERSEN MAKE ME HAPPY TO DAY

DRAW SOMETHING AWESOME THAT HAPPEND TO DAY

DATE: MO TU WE TH FR SR ...../...../......

TO DAY I AM THANKFUL FOR

1

....
....

3

....
....

2

....
....

THI PERSEN MAKE ME HAPPY TO DAY

....

DRAW SOMETHING AWESOME THAT HAPPEND TO DAY

DATE: MO TU WE TH FR SR ...../..../......

TO DAY I AM THANKFUL FOR

• • • • • • • • • • • • • • • • • • • •

1

....

....

3

....

....

2

....

....

I FEEL

THI PERSEN MAKE ME HAPPY TO DAY

....

DRAW SOMETHING AWESOME THAT HAPPEND TO DAY

DATE: MO TU WE TH FR SR ..../..../......

TO DAY I AM THANKFUL FOR

1

3

2

I FEEL

THI PERSEN MAKE ME HAPPY TO DAY

DRAW SOMETHING AWESOME THAT HAPPEND TO DAY

DATE: MO TU WE TH FR SR ..../..../......

TO DAY I AM THANKFUL FOR

1

....

....

3

....

....

2

....

....

I FEEL

THI PERSEN MAKE ME HAPPY TO DAY

....

DRAW SOMETHING AWESOME THAT HAPPEND TO DAY

DATE: MO TU WE TH FR SR ...../..../......

TO DAY I AM THANKFUL FOR

1

....
....

3

....
....

2

....
....

I FEEL

THI PERSEN MAKE ME HAPPY TO DAY

....

DRAW SOMETHING AWESOME THAT HAPPEND TO DAY

DATE: MO TU WE TH FR SR ...../..../......

TO DAY I AM THANKFUL FOR

THI PERSEN MAKE ME HAPPY TO DAY

DRAW SOMETHING AWESOME THAT HAPPEND TO DAY

DATE: MO TU WE TH FR SR ...../..../......

TO DAY I AM THANKFUL FOR

1

3

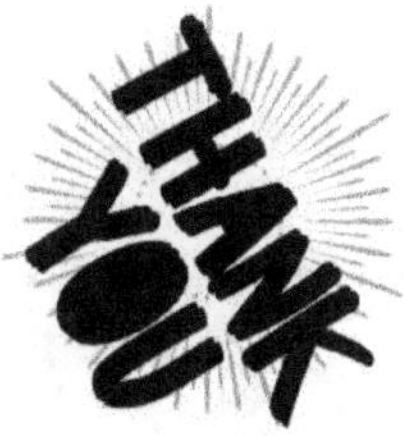

2

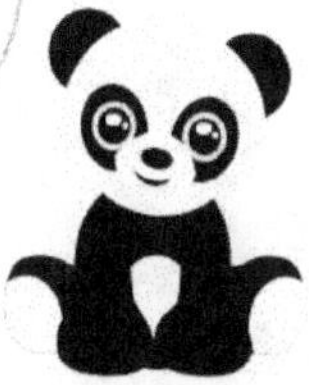

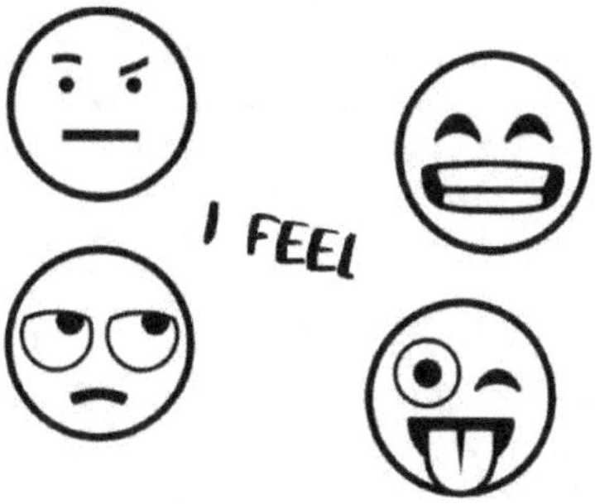

THI PERSEN MAKE ME HAPPY TO DAY

....

DRAW SOMETHING AWESOME THAT HAPPEND TO DAY

DATE: MO TU WE TH FR SR ...../..../......

TO DAY I AM THANKFUL FOR

THI PERSEN MAKE ME HAPPY TO DAY

DRAW SOMETHING AWESOME THAT HAPPEND TO DAY

DATE: MO TU WE TH FR SR ...../..../......

TO DAY I AM THANKFUL FOR

1

3

2

THI PERSEN MAKE ME HAPPY TO DAY

DRAW SOMETHING AWESOME THAT HAPPEND TO DAY

DATE: MO TU WE TH FR SR ...../..../.......

TO DAY I AM THANKFUL FOR

1

....

....

3

....

....

2

....

....

I FEEL

THI PERSEN MAKE ME HAPPY TO DAY

....

DRAW SOMETHING AWESOME THAT HAPPEND TO DAY

TO DAY I AM THANKFUL FOR

1

3

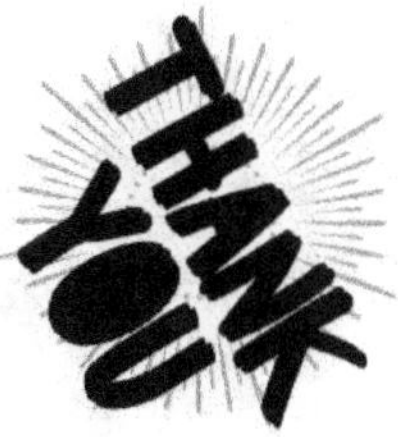

2

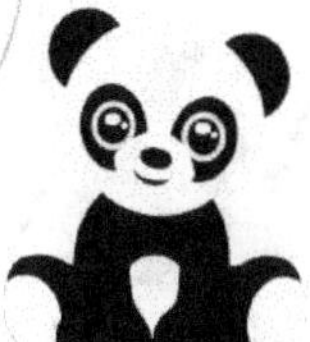

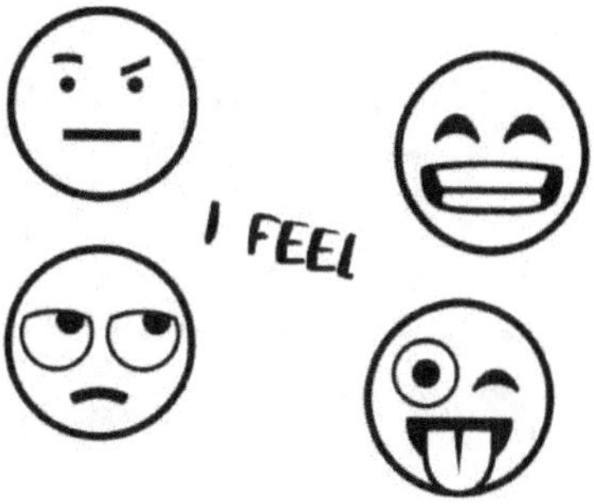

I FEEL

THI PERSEN MAKE ME HAPPY TO DAY

DRAW SOMETHING AWESOME THAT HAPPEND TO DAY

DATE: MO TU WE TH FR SR ...../..../......

TO DAY I AM THANKFUL FOR

1

....

....

3

....

....

2

....

....

I FEEL

THI PERSEN MAKE ME HAPPY TO DAY

....

DRAW SOMETHING AWESOME THAT HAPPEND TO DAY

DATE: MO TU WE TH FR SR ...../..../......

TO DAY I AM THANKFUL FOR

1

....
....

3

....
....

2

....
....

I FEEL

THI PERSEN MAKE ME HAPPY TO DAY

....

DRAW SOMETHING AWESOME THAT HAPPEND TO DAY

DATE: MO TU WE TH FR SR ...../..../......

TO DAY I AM THANKFUL FOR

1

....
....

3

....
....

2

....
....

I FEEL

THI PERSEN MAKE ME HAPPY TO DAY

....

DRAW SOMETHING AWESOME THAT HAPPEND TO DAY

DATE: MO TU WE TH FR SR ...../..../......

TO DAY I AM THANKFUL FOR

1

....
....

3

....
....

2

....
....

I FEEL

THI PERSEN MAKE ME HAPPY TO DAY

....

DRAW SOMETHING AWESOME THAT HAPPEND TO DAY

DATE: MO TU WE TH FR SR ...../..../.......

TO DAY I AM THANKFUL FOR

1

3

2

I FEEL

THI PERSEN MAKE ME HAPPY TO DAY

DRAW SOMETHING AWESOME THAT HAPPEND TO DAY

DATE: MO TU WE TH FR SR ...../...../......

TO DAY I AM THANKFUL FOR

1

3

2

I FEEL

THI PERSEN MAKE ME HAPPY TO DAY

DRAW SOMETHING AWESOME THAT HAPPEND TO DAY

DATE: MO TU WE TH FR SR ...../..../......

TO DAY I AM THANKFUL FOR

1

3

2

I FEEL

THI PERSEN MAKE ME HAPPY TO DAY

DRAW SOMETHING AWESOME THAT HAPPEND TO DAY

DATE: MO TU WE TH FR SR ...../..../.......

TO DAY I AM THANKFUL FOR

1

....
....

3

....
....

2

....
....

I FEEL

THI PERSEN MAKE ME HAPPY TO DAY

....

DRAW SOMETHING AWESOME THAT HAPPEND TO DAY

DATE: MO TU WE TH FR SR ...../..../......

TO DAY I AM THANKFUL FOR

1

3

....
....

....
....

2

....
....

I FEEL

THI PERSEN MAKE ME HAPPY TO DAY
....

DRAW SOMETHING AWESOME THAT HAPPEND TO DAY

DATE: MO TU WE TH FR SR ...../..../......

TO DAY I AM THANKFUL FOR

1

....

....

3

....

....

2

....

....

I FEEL

THI PERSEN MAKE ME HAPPY TO DAY

....

DRAW SOMETHING AWESOME THAT HAPPEND TO DAY

DATE: MO TU WE TH FR SR ...../..../........

TO DAY I AM THANKFUL FOR

1

....

....

3

....

....

2

....

....

I FEEL

THI PERSEN MAKE ME HAPPY TO DAY

....

DRAW SOMETHING AWESOME THAT HAPPEND TO DAY

DATE: MO TU WE TH FR SR ...../.../......

TO DAY I AM THANKFUL FOR

1

3

2

THI PERSEN MAKE ME HAPPY TO DAY

DRAW SOMETHING AWESOME THAT HAPPEND TO DAY

DATE: MO TU WE TH FR SR ....../...../......

TO DAY I AM THANKFUL FOR

1

3

2

THI PERSEN MAKE ME HAPPY TO DAY

DRAW SOMETHING AWESOME THAT HAPPEND TO DAY

DATE: MO TU WE TH FR SR ..…/..…/..……

TO DAY I AM THANKFUL FOR

1

....
....

3

....
....

2

....
....

THI PERSEN MAKE ME HAPPY TO DAY

....

DRAW SOMETHING AWESOME THAT HAPPEND TO DAY

DATE: MO TU WE TH FR SR ...../..../......

TO DAY I AM THANKFUL FOR

THI PERSEN MAKE ME HAPPY TO DAY

DRAW SOMETHING AWESOME THAT HAPPEND TO DAY

DATE: MO TU WE TH FR SR ...../..../......

TO DAY I AM THANKFUL FOR

1

3

2

THI PERSEN MAKE ME HAPPY TO DAY

DRAW SOMETHING AWESOME THAT HAPPEND TO DAY

DATE: MO TU WE TH FR SR ...../..../.......

TO DAY I AM THANKFUL FOR

1

3

....
....

....
....

2

....
....

I FEEL

THI PERSEN MAKE ME HAPPY TO DAY 

....

DRAW SOMETHING AWESOME THAT HAPPEND TO DAY

DATE: MO TU WE TH FR SR ...../..../......

TO DAY I AM THANKFUL FOR

• • • • • • • • • • • • • • • • • • • •

1

....
....

3

....
....

2

....
....

I FEEL

THI PERSEN MAKE ME HAPPY TO DAY 

....

DRAW SOMETHING AWESOME THAT HAPPEND TO DAY

DATE: MO TU WE TH FR SR ...../..../......

TO DAY I AM THANKFUL FOR

1

3

THANK YOU

2

I FEEL

THI PERSEN MAKE ME HAPPY TO DAY

DRAW SOMETHING AWESOME THAT HAPPEND TO DAY

DATE: MO TU WE TH FR SR ..../..../......

TO DAY I AM THANKFUL FOR

● ● ● ● ● ● ● ● ● ● ● ● ● ● ● ● ● ● ● ●

THI PERSEN MAKE ME HAPPY TO DAY

DRAW SOMETHING AWESOME THAT HAPPEND TO DAY

DATE: MO TU WE TH FR SR ...../..../......

TO DAY I AM THANKFUL FOR

1

3

....
....

....
....

2

....
....

I FEEL

THI PERSEN MAKE ME HAPPY TO DAY

....

DRAW SOMETHING AWESOME THAT HAPPEND TO DAY

DATE: MO TU WE TH FR SR ...../...../......

TO DAY I AM THANKFUL FOR

1

3

....
....

....
....

2

....
....

THI PERSEN MAKE ME HAPPY TO DAY

....

DRAW SOMETHING AWESOME THAT HAPPEND TO DAY

DATE: MO TU WE TH FR SR ...../...../......

TO DAY I AM THANKFUL FOR

● ● ● ● ● ● ● ● ● ● ● ● ● ● ● ● ● ● ●

1

....
....

3

....
....

2

....
....

I FEEL

THI PERSEN MAKE ME HAPPY TO DAY

....

DRAW SOMETHING AWESOME THAT HAPPEND TO DAY

DATE: MO TU WE TH FR SR ...../..../......

TO DAY I AM THANKFUL FOR

1

3

....

....

....

....

2

....

....

I FEEL

THI PERSEN MAKE ME HAPPY TO DAY

....

DRAW SOMETHING AWESOME THAT HAPPEND TO DAY

DATE: MO TU WE TH FR SR ...../...../......

TO DAY I AM THANKFUL FOR

1

3

2

I FEEL

THI PERSEN MAKE ME HAPPY TO DAY

DRAW SOMETHING AWESOME THAT HAPPEND TO DAY

DATE: MO TU WE TH FR SR ...../..../......

TO DAY I AM THANKFUL FOR

1

3

2

THI PERSEN MAKE ME HAPPY TO DAY

DRAW SOMETHING AWESOME THAT HAPPEND TO DAY

DATE: MO TU WE TH FR SR ...../...../......

TO DAY I AM THANKFUL FOR

THI PERSEN MAKE ME HAPPY TO DAY

DRAW SOMETHING AWESOME THAT HAPPEND TO DAY

DATE: MO TU WE TH FR SR ...../...../......

TO DAY I AM THANKFUL FOR

1

3

....
....

....
....

2

....
....

I FEEL

THI PERSEN MAKE ME HAPPY TO DAY

DRAW SOMETHING AWESOME THAT HAPPEND TO DAY

DATE: MO TU WE TH FR SR ...../...../.......

TO DAY I AM THANKFUL FOR

1

....

....

3

THANK YOU

....

....

2

....

....

I FEEL

THI PERSEN MAKE ME HAPPY TO DAY

....

DRAW SOMETHING AWESOME THAT HAPPEND TO DAY

DATE: MO TU WE TH FR SR ...../..../......

TO DAY I AM THANKFUL FOR

1

3

2

THI PERSEN MAKE ME HAPPY TO DAY

....

DRAW SOMETHING AWESOME THAT HAPPEND TO DAY

DATE: MO TU WE TH FR SR ...../..../......

TO DAY I AM THANKFUL FOR

THI PERSEN MAKE ME HAPPY TO DAY

DRAW SOMETHING AWESOME THAT HAPPEND TO DAY

DATE: MO TU WE TH FR SR ...../..../......

TO DAY I AM THANKFUL FOR

1

3

2

I FEEL

THI PERSEN MAKE ME HAPPY TO DAY

DRAW SOMETHING AWESOME THAT HAPPEND TO DAY

DATE: MO TU WE TH FR SR ...../...../......

TO DAY I AM THANKFUL FOR

THI PERSEN MAKE ME HAPPY TO DAY

DRAW SOMETHING AWESOME THAT HAPPEND TO DAY

DATE: MO TU WE TH FR SR ...../..../......

TO DAY I AM THANKFUL FOR

1

3

2

THI PERSEN MAKE ME HAPPY TO DAY

DRAW SOMETHING AWESOME THAT HAPPEND TO DAY

DATE: MO TU WE TH FR SR ...../...../.......

TO DAY I AM THANKFUL FOR

1

....
....

3

....
....

2

....
....

THI PERSEN MAKE ME HAPPY TO DAY

....

DRAW SOMETHING AWESOME THAT HAPPEND TO DAY

DATE: MO TU WE TH FR SR ...../...../......

TO DAY I AM THANKFUL FOR

1

3

2

THI PERSEN MAKE ME HAPPY TO DAY

....

DRAW SOMETHING AWESOME THAT HAPPEND TO DAY

DATE: MO TU WE TH FR SR ....../...../......

TO DAY I AM THANKFUL FOR

1

3

2

I FEEL

THI PERSEN MAKE ME HAPPY TO DAY

DRAW SOMETHING AWESOME THAT HAPPEND TO DAY

DATE: MO TU WE TH FR SR ...../.../......

TO DAY I AM THANKFUL FOR

1

....
....

3

....
....

2

....
....

I FEEL

THI PERSEN MAKE ME HAPPY TO DAY

....

DRAW SOMETHING AWESOME THAT HAPPEND TO DAY

DATE: MO TU WE TH FR SR ...../..../......

TO DAY I AM THANKFUL FOR

1

....
....

3

....
....

2

....
....

I FEEL

THI PERSEN MAKE ME HAPPY TO DAY

....

DRAW SOMETHING AWESOME THAT HAPPEND TO DAY

DATE: MO TU WE TH FR SR ...../..../......

TO DAY I AM THANKFUL FOR

1

3

2

I FEEL

THI PERSEN MAKE ME HAPPY TO DAY

....

DRAW SOMETHING AWESOME THAT HAPPEND TO DAY

DATE: MO TU WE TH FR SR ...../..../.......

TO DAY I AM THANKFUL FOR

1

3

2

I FEEL

THI PERSEN MAKE ME HAPPY TO DAY

DRAW SOMETHING AWESOME THAT HAPPEND TO DAY

DATE: MO TU WE TH FR SR ..../..../......

TO DAY I AM THANKFUL FOR

1

....
....

3

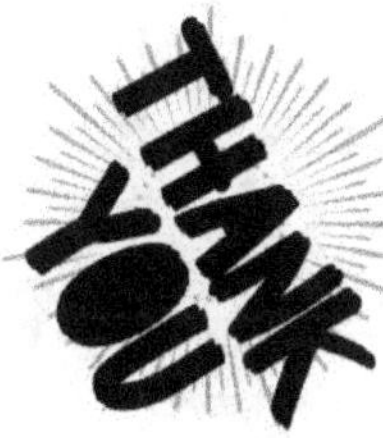

....
....

2

....
....

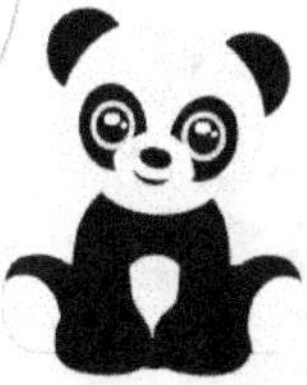

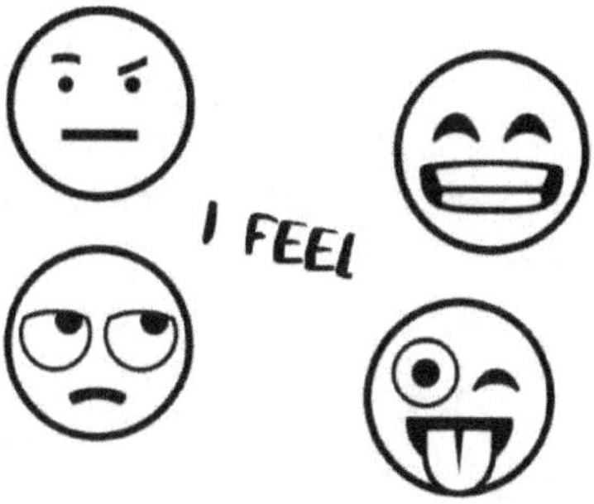

I FEEL

THI PERSEN MAKE ME HAPPY TO DAY

....

DRAW SOMETHING AWESOME THAT HAPPEND TO DAY

....

DATE: MO TU WE TH FR SR ...../...../......

TO DAY I AM THANKFUL FOR

THI PERSEN MAKE ME HAPPY TO DAY

DRAW SOMETHING AWESOME THAT HAPPEND TO DAY

DATE: MO TU WE TH FR SR ..../..../......

TO DAY I AM THANKFUL FOR

1

3

....
....

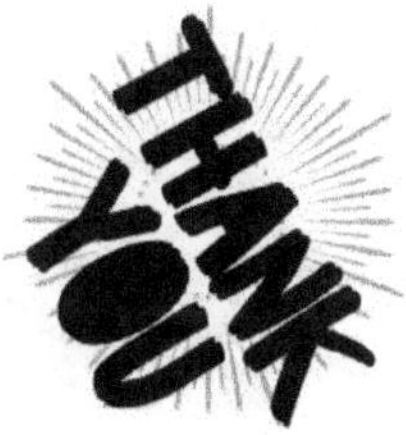

....
....

2

....
....

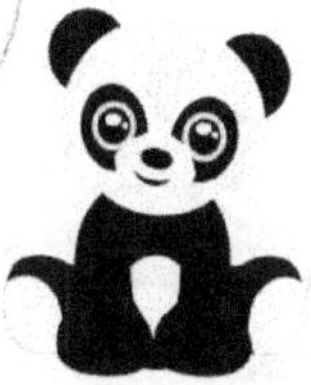

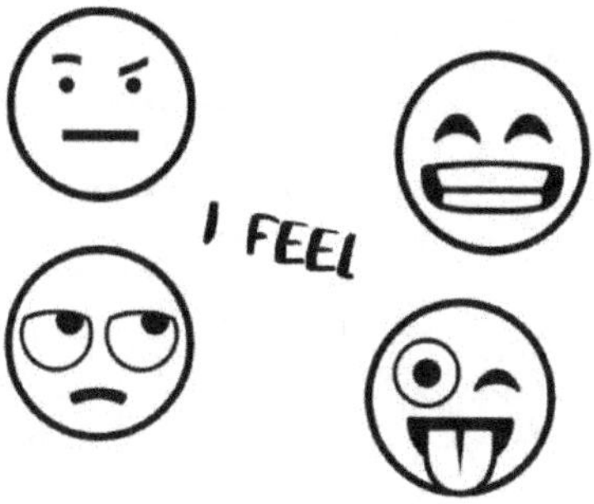

I FEEL

THI PERSEN MAKE ME HAPPY TO DAY

....

DRAW SOMETHING AWESOME THAT HAPPEND TO DAY

DATE: MO TU WE TH FR SR ...../..../......

TO DAY I AM THANKFUL FOR

1

3

2

THI PERSEN MAKE ME HAPPY TO DAY

....

DRAW SOMETHING AWESOME THAT HAPPEND TO DAY

DATE: MO TU WE TH FR SR ...../..../......

TO DAY I AM THANKFUL FOR

1

3

....
....

....
....

2

....
....

THI PERSEN MAKE ME HAPPY TO DAY

....

DRAW SOMETHING AWESOME THAT HAPPEND TO DAY

DATE: MO TU WE TH FR SR ...../...../.......

TO DAY I AM THANKFUL FOR

1

3

....
....

....
....

2

....
....

I FEEL

THI PERSEN MAKE ME HAPPY TO DAY

....

DRAW SOMETHING AWESOME THAT HAPPEND TO DAY

DATE: MO TU WE TH FR SR ...../..../......

TO DAY I AM THANKFUL FOR

1

3

2

THI PERSEN MAKE ME HAPPY TO DAY

DRAW SOMETHING AWESOME THAT HAPPEND TO DAY

DATE: MO TU WE TH FR SR ....../....../......

TO DAY I AM THANKFUL FOR

1

3

2

THI PERSEN MAKE ME HAPPY TO DAY

DRAW SOMETHING AWESOME THAT HAPPEND TO DAY

DATE: MO TU WE TH FR SR ...../...../......

TO DAY I AM THANKFUL FOR

1

3

2

THI PERSEN MAKE ME HAPPY TO DAY

DRAW SOMETHING AWESOME THAT HAPPEND TO DAY

DATE: MO TU WE TH FR SR ...../..../.......

TO DAY I AM THANKFUL FOR

1

....

....

3

....

....

2

....

....

I FEEL

THI PERSEN MAKE ME HAPPY TO DAY

....

DRAW SOMETHING AWESOME THAT HAPPEND TO DAY

DATE: MO TU WE TH FR SR ...../..../......

TO DAY I AM THANKFUL FOR

1

3

2

I FEEL

THI PERSEN MAKE ME HAPPY TO DAY

DRAW SOMETHING AWESOME THAT HAPPEND TO DAY

DATE: MO TU WE TH FR SR ...../..../.......

TO DAY I AM THANKFUL FOR

1

....
....

3

....
....

2

....
....

I FEEL

THI PERSEN MAKE ME HAPPY TO DAY

....

DRAW SOMETHING AWESOME THAT HAPPEND TO DAY

DATE: MO TU WE TH FR SR ...../..../......

TO DAY I AM THANKFUL FOR

1

3

2

I FEEL

THI PERSEN MAKE ME HAPPY TO DAY

DRAW SOMETHING AWESOME THAT HAPPEND TO DAY

DATE: MO TU WE TH FR SR ...../..../......

TO DAY I AM THANKFUL FOR

1

....
....

3

....
....

2

....
....

I FEEL

THI PERSEN MAKE ME HAPPY TO DAY

....

DRAW SOMETHING AWESOME THAT HAPPEND TO DAY

DATE: MO TU WE TH FR SR ..../..../......

TO DAY I AM THANKFUL FOR

1

3

THANK YOU

2

I FEEL

THI PERSEN MAKE ME HAPPY TO DAY

DRAW SOMETHING AWESOME THAT HAPPEND TO DAY

DATE: MO TU WE TH FR SR ...../..../......

TO DAY I AM THANKFUL FOR

THI PERSEN MAKE ME HAPPY TO DAY

DRAW SOMETHING AWESOME THAT HAPPEND TO DAY

DATE: MO TU WE TH FR SR ...../...../......

TO DAY I AM THANKFUL FOR

1

3

....
....

....
....

2

....
....

I FEEL

THI PERSEN MAKE ME HAPPY TO DAY

DRAW SOMETHING AWESOME THAT HAPPEND TO DAY

DATE: MO TU WE TH FR SR ....../....../........

TO DAY I AM THANKFUL FOR

1

....

....

3

....

....

2

....

....

I FEEL

THI PERSEN MAKE ME HAPPY TO DAY

....

DRAW SOMETHING AWESOME THAT HAPPEND TO DAY

DATE: MO TU WE TH FR SR ...../..../......

TO DAY I AM THANKFUL FOR

1

3

2

I FEEL

THI PERSEN MAKE ME HAPPY TO DAY

....

DRAW SOMETHING AWESOME THAT HAPPEND TO DAY

DATE: MO TU WE TH FR SR ...../...../......

TO DAY I AM THANKFUL FOR

1

3

2

THI PERSEN MAKE ME HAPPY TO DAY

....

DRAW SOMETHING AWESOME THAT HAPPEND TO DAY

DATE: MO TU WE TH FR SR ...../..../......

TO DAY I AM THANKFUL FOR

● ● ● ● ● ● ● ● ● ● ● ● ● ● ● ● ● ● ●

1

3

....
....

....
....

2

....
....

I FEEL

THI PERSEN MAKE ME HAPPY TO DAY

....

DRAW SOMETHING AWESOME THAT HAPPEND TO DAY

DATE: MO TU WE TH FR SR ...../..../.......

TO DAY I AM THANKFUL FOR

1

3

2

THI PERSEN MAKE ME HAPPY TO DAY

DRAW SOMETHING AWESOME THAT HAPPEND TO DAY

DATE: MO TU WE TH FR SR ....../...../......

TO DAY I AM THANKFUL FOR

1

3

....
....

....
....

2

....
....

I FEEL

THI PERSEN MAKE ME HAPPY TO DAY

....

DRAW SOMETHING AWESOME THAT HAPPEND TO DAY

DATE: MO TU WE TH FR SR ...../..../.......

TO DAY I AM THANKFUL FOR

1

....
....

3

....
....

2

....
....

I FEEL

THI PERSEN MAKE ME HAPPY TO DAY

....

DRAW SOMETHING AWESOME THAT HAPPEND TO DAY

DATE: MO TU WE TH FR SR ...../..../......

TO DAY I AM THANKFUL FOR

1

3

2

I FEEL

THI PERSEN MAKE ME HAPPY TO DAY

DRAW SOMETHING AWESOME THAT HAPPEND TO DAY

DATE: MO TU WE TH FR SR ...../..../......

TO DAY I AM THANKFUL FOR

1

3

2

THANK YOU

I FEEL

THI PERSEN MAKE ME HAPPY TO DAY

DRAW SOMETHING AWESOME THAT HAPPEND TO DAY

DATE: MO TU WE TH FR SR ..../..../......

TO DAY I AM THANKFUL FOR

1

....

....

3

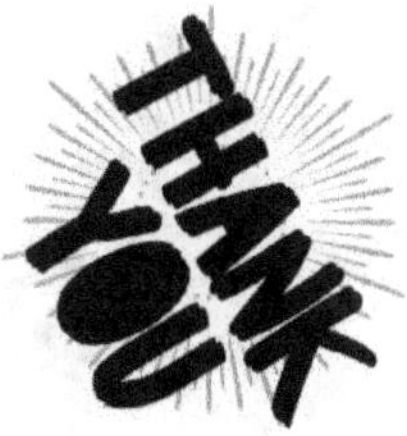

....

....

2

....

....

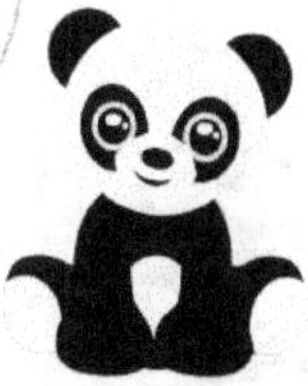

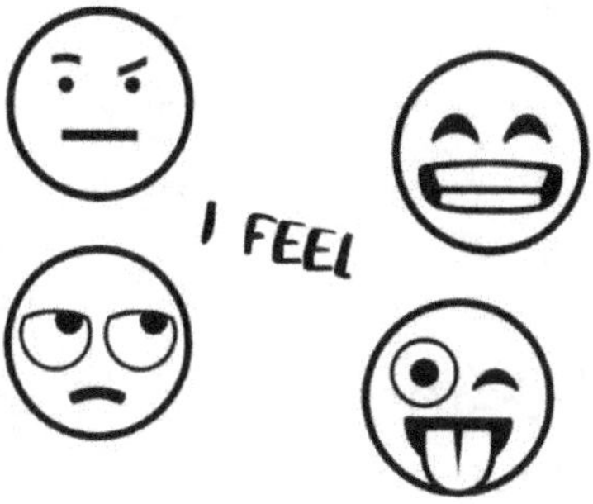

I FEEL

THI PERSEN MAKE ME HAPPY TO DAY

....

DRAW SOMETHING AWESOME THAT HAPPEND TO DAY

DATE: MO TU WE TH FR SR ...../...../.......

TO DAY I AM THANKFUL FOR

1

3

2

THI PERSEN MAKE ME HAPPY TO DAY

DRAW SOMETHING AWESOME THAT HAPPEND TO DAY

DATE: MO TU WE TH FR SR ...../..../.......

TO DAY I AM THANKFUL FOR

1

....
....

3

....
....

2

....
....

I FEEL

THI PERSEN MAKE ME HAPPY TO DAY

DRAW SOMETHING AWESOME THAT HAPPEND TO DAY

DATE: MO TU WE TH FR SR ...../..../.......

TO DAY I AM THANKFUL FOR

1

3

....

....

....

....

2

....

....

I FEEL

THI PERSEN MAKE ME HAPPY TO DAY

DRAW SOMETHING AWESOME THAT HAPPEND TO DAY